Corporate Fairy Tales

Paul A Brodsky

IMOCO Publishing
Tulsa, OK
USA

Corporate Fairy Tales
By Paul Brodsky

Published by:
    IMOCO Publishing
    P.O. Box 471721
    Tulsa, OK 74147-1721
    Email: IMOCO@AOL.COM

Copyright © 1998 by Paul Brodsky

All rights reserved. No part of this book may be reproduced or transmitted in any form or by any means, electronic or mechanical, including photocopying, recording by any information storage and retrieval system without written permission from the author, except for the inclusion of brief quotations in a review.

ISBN 0-9661165-5-0
Library of Congress Catalog Number: 97-97098

DEDICATION
To my parents, who got me through the first part of life and to my wife, who will help me through the rest.

IN MEMORY
Of my Grandmother Brodsky - your dinosaur grandson finally did it.

SPECIAL THANKS
To my friends, who listened to my ideas, gave me great support and suggestions, and basically told me to get off my rear and do it already.

This page intentionally contains only this line.

Table of Contents

The Three Little Webmasters 9
Goldstein and the Three Lawyers 17
The Pied Piper of Excellence 23
The Three Applicants to Gruff 29
Little Red's Riding Hoods 35
The Lowly Employee 43
The Little Accountant That Could 49
Assorted Rhymes and Poems 53

So what do you think of the book so far? Pretty gripping stuff.

How about that copyright page? Simply amazing. And the dedication page.....quite a tear jerker.

Introduction

Growing up, almost all of us are exposed to the standard stock of children's stories, songs, and rhymes. These stories do a wonderful job of preparing us for some of life's challenges. For example, from the great story of the Three Little Pigs, we learn a valuable lesson about choosing proper home building materials particularly when locating in an area prone to high winds.

It is through the teachings of Little Red Riding Hood that we realize the extreme importance of today's stalking laws. And let us not forget the poor woman who lives in a shoe. Her tragic saga serves as a constant reminder that there are those in life less fortunate than us.

Without these valuable stories, we would no doubt be a less advanced society. However, the sad truth is that they do nothing to prepare us for the cruel, though ever rewarding, world of business. There has been speculation that this tremendous gap in American literature was one of the key elements that led to the great depression of the 1920's.

Think of all the kids out there who open up a lemonade stand without first developing a business plan or implementing a quality program. If you have ever wondered why so many of these young entrepreneurs are forced to shut down business within hours of opening, it's because they don't have the proper educational resources.

It is for this reason that I felt compelled to write this book. It is my hope that this simple collection of prose will help many generations prepare for, or deal with, the harsh realities of a dog-eat-dog world in a fun and entertaining way.

The Three Little Webmasters

Once upon a time, an incredible phenomenon occurred. Three programmers at three different companies had the same idea at the same time.

"Hey!", they thought. "We should put our company on the Internet!"

This kind of thinking was so unique, unusual, and profound, it was a moral imperative that a story be written about it. So sit back, relax, and prepare yourself to absorb the high level lessons that are presented in this story. Don't worry if you don't get it the first time. We are certain that a Cliff Notes version will be available soon.

And now, because I know you can't wait any longer, the story begins...

So these three programmers decided to put their companies on the Internet and the World Wide Web. After snowing over upper management with a huge amount of technobabble, they won approval and were elevated to the status of Webmaster. A Webmaster is just like a programmer except they know that Java is more than just fancy coffee. This supreme knowledge allows them to command a much higher salary than your average programmer.

So anyhow, the first little Webmaster set out to put his company on the Internet. He was in such a hurry to make their presence known that he went out and bought the cheapest and easiest thing he could find.

All the vendors kept telling him, "Beware the big bad hackers. They will stop at nothing to get your data."

The first little Webmaster didn't listen and went

ahead with his plans. One day while he was downloading pictures off the internet for a self-motivated 'human anatomy' study, a message appeared across the screen.

"Little Webmaster, Little Webmaster, let me have access," said the Big Bad Hacker.

"Not by the space that's left on my hard driveus," said the first little Webmaster.

(author's note: I know driveus isn't a word but it was the only thing I could think of that rhymes with access)

"Then I'll hack, and I'll byte, and I'll CRASH your whole system!" said the Big Bad Hacker. And in a flash the Big Bad Hacker brought down their whole system.

The second little Webmaster was a little smarter than the first and knew he had to implement some security measures to protect their system. He was feeling so secure that he spent most of his days playing 'Doom' across the Internet with a Webmaster in another country. One day, just as he was about to blow away his opponent, a message appeared across the screen.

"Little Webmaster, Little Webmaster, let me see your file," said the Big Bad Hacker.

"Not by all the water in the Nile!" said the second little Webmaster. (I know that doesn't make much sense, but in real life things seldom do.)

"Than I'll hack, and I'll byte, and I'll crash your whole system," said the Big Bad Hacker. The second little Webmaster had put in some fairly good security and it took the Hacker nearly twice as long to crash the system (about 10 minutes) but crash it he did.

The third little Webmaster was smart enough to know that security was not an issue to be taken lightly. He took extra precautions by using an external server, a firewall, and lots of other technical junk that most people don't understand (or don't care to understand.)

Sure enough, one day while he was running a Level 1 Diagnostic on the system (all the Trekkies know what a Level 1 Diagnostic is, just ask them), a message appeared across the screen.

"Little Webmaster, Little Webmaster, let me see your drives!" said the Big Bad Hacker.

"Give it a shot, you've got three tries," said the third Little Webmaster.

The Big Bad Hacker hacked, and bit, and bit, and hacked but he was unable to break into the system. After the allotted three tries, the third Little Webmaster pressed the "any" key and sent a virus back through the Internet that exploded the hacker's computer (now you know what that key is for.) The third little Webmaster had been victorious and became a highly trusted and respected employee.

The Moral Of The Story

Normally you would assume that the moral of this story is that if you put in the time and effort to keep your web site secure, you will benefit greatly. However, I fear that most people are only thinking, "Hmm, I think I would like to conduct my own 'human anatomy' study."

Epilogue

Now you're probably wondering what happened to the three Little Webmasters. The first Little Webmaster never quite got the hang of creating web pages. Eventually he opened a little cafe where people could come and use computers to access the Internet. Their famous line was, "How about a little Java with your Java?"

The second Little Webmaster was able to convince his management that due to their lack of attentiveness and funding to their Internet project, security was breached. Senior Management felt so badly that they made him the VP over "Research of Emerging Technologies." Tough job.

The third Little Webmaster was looked upon so highly by Senior Management that he was promoted and given full security access to corporate data. Unfortunately, he could not handle that kind of responsibility. He allowed himself to be coerced into giving away proprietary corporate data in exchange for pre-release copies of video games. Currently, he is serving time in a medium security facility, but still has Internet access.

The authorities eventually caught the Big Bad Hacker. He was last heard from shortly before the CIA picked him up. It is believed that he is now working on some top-secret project under a mountain somewhere. The CIA will neither confirm nor deny the existence of such a facility.

Feel free to photocopy this page and use it for notes. Or, if you prefer, use this page to write a note to the author telling him how wonderful the book is.

Goldstein and the Three Lawyers

s far as you're concerned, the following story is true but the names and facts have been changed so they in no way resemble anyone you know. However, if any of the characters in this story appear to be someone you know, they probably are. The coincidence will be too great to ignore and you should act upon it immediately in an appropriate manner.

Once upon a time, in a land far far away, where the corporate world is a tough, brutal, environment and internal politics are an everyday battle, (OK, so maybe it's not so far away) there were three lawyers; Papasky, Mamartin, and Baborski.

On this particular day they were hard at work (uh.....yeah) lawyering or whatever it is that lawyers do when they're not appearing on Court TV. Suddenly, they decided to go off and have their usual three-martini power lunch and maybe chase some ambulances for exercise.

Not long after they had gone, Rubin Goldstein, an energetic new recruit from the mailroom, came by looking for extra interoffice envelopes so he could send out a chain letter. Upon entering the reception area of the lawyer's offices he noticed that everyone was gone and thought this would be a good opportunity to learn more about this crazy, clear cut, precise world that we call the 'writ of habeas corpus' (because that sounds better than just saying law).

The first thing young Goldstein noticed was the three diplomas hanging on the wall. All the major universities were represented. The Evelyn Wood School of Law (you get your degree in half the time), The Congressional School of Ethical Law, and the Emanuel Kant School of Legal Awareness.

After staring in awe of the diplomas for a while, Goldstein noticed that they all seemed to be a little crooked (.....think about it.....). Being the spunky young lad that he was, he decided to straighten them out a bit (something we would all like to see happen). The first two were easy to fix but as soon as he touched the third, it fell off the wall and the frame broke. Not sure what to do, he just left it and moved on.

Goldstein then went into the conference room where the lawyers had been um....working (hee hee, that always cracks me up). There he saw three stacks of papers. "Golly! What have we here?" he thought to himself (since no one else was in the room).

Goldstein started looking over the papers. While perusing over the last stack, he got so alarmed at something he saw, he jumped up and accidentally spilled some coffee all over the papers. Still not sure what to do he just left it and moved on.

Next, he entered the offices of the three lawyers. Here, he found all kinds of information; files, tape recordings, photographs, and other juicy stuff. Goldstein decided to begin doing some "research."

By this time, the three lawyers had returned from their lunch. Upon entering the lobby, their keen instincts told them something just wasn't quite right.

"Hey!" exclaimed Papasky, "someone's been messing with my diploma!"

"Someone's been messing with my diploma too!" yelled Mamartin.

"All you guys ever do is complain about stupid stuff!" cried Baborski. "Someone has been messing with my diploma and it's broken all over the floor."

In typical lawyer fashion they moved slowly (..think about it again..) into the conference room.

"Someone has been playing with my briefs!" said Papasky.

"I like it when someone plays with my briefs.....um.....I mean....HEY, someone has been playing with my briefs too!" said Mamartin.

"You guys are such losers!" said Baborski. "Someone has been playing with my briefs and spilled coffee all over them. Do you realize how many additional hours I will have to bill to my client while I have a paralegal fix them?"

Next they moved into the offices where they found Goldstein who was just completing his "research." Before any of them could say a word, Goldstein glared at them and said,

"I have enough information here to put you all away for a long time. Unless of course you are willing to plea bargain a deal!"

The three lawyers knew they had been subjugated

(which is a lawyer type term for beaten) so they decided to settle by making Goldstein a full partner in the firm.

And thus began the long rein of Papasky, Mamartin, Baborski, and Goldstein who later became known in the legal world as simply, "The Firm."

The Pied Piper
of Excellence

nce upon a time there was a company called Hamelin Inc. Hamelin Inc. was an ordinary company going about its business in these modern times. Business was brisk, profit margins were high, and the customers were happy. Fortunately, Hamelin Inc. had a president who was smart enough to know that this could only mean trouble was afoot and it was time to call for help.

So, after reading an article in *Business Fad Weekly* and consulting with his next door neighbor, the President of Hamelin Inc. called the one person qualified to transform the company into the bureaucratic operation it should be. He called the Pied Piper of Excellence.

The Pied Piper of Excellence was a strange and mysterious fellow. He was always immaculately dressed and spoke a strange language made up mostly of acronyms.

"Pied Piper of Excellence," said the President. "We need you to rid our company of all the bad things and magically transform us into a higher being."

"No problem," said the Pied Piper of Excellence. "However, you must promise to continue to pay me for years to come while I guide your company on its heuristic journey down the path of Excellence."

"Yes, I promise," said the President.

And so with a quasi-legally binding contract in hand, the Pied Piper of Excellence set about his work. He worked long and hard to transform the employees of Hamelin Inc. from the unproductive and defect laden individuals they were into lean, mean, measurement machines.

The employees were quickly learning about this wonderful new tool called Excellence. In no time at all, they were producing charts, drawing arrows, and wearing buttons with wonderfully inspirational sayings on them. Some of the more advanced employees were even able to accurately measure the amount of time they spent measuring their measurable activities. The impact on employee moral was indescribable.

Soon the effect of the excellence program was apparent. No work was done without first creating a series of useful and intensely detailed flow charts that took hundreds of work hours at enormous expense to complete (that's how we know they're good). Request forms were also required before any work could be done, no matter how small or mundane the task.

For example, there was a request form that was to be completed to request additional request forms so that work could be requested. This worked well except for the rare occasion that a form changed. In this case, you would need to complete a form to request new request forms so you could then request that the old forms be disposed of.

In other words, the program had been a complete success. The President of Hamelin Inc. met once again with the Pied Piper of Excellence.

"Pied Piper of Excellence," said the President. "The program is going so well, I have decided that we no longer need your services. Our employees are so immersed in Excellence that they have lost sight of what products we sell. We have lost so many customers that we will soon be able to completely eliminate our customer service department. The reduction in staff will save hundreds of thousands of dollars per year. Thank you for what you have done but I believe we can continue the program without you."

"You'll pay for this!" shouted the Pied Piper of

Excellence.

"Don't go away mad," said the President. "Please, take this pen with our company name and logo on it as a token of our appreciation."

The Pied Piper of Excellence was furious. In a rage he pulled one more very dangerous tool of Excellence from his attaché case... **EMPOWERMENT**. He ran amok (fun word, "amok") through the company spreading **EMPOWERMENT** to the employees. Soon the entire company was broken up into strategic business units and all the employees had formed self-directed work groups. The customers were back, sales were up, and the shareholders were once again questioning executive level spending. It was total anarchy.

The President knew he had been beaten. The Pied Piper of Excellence eventually disappeared, but we often hear tales of how he is simply waiting in the shadows, developing his next evil plot.

While I am certain that the above story may seem vaguely familiar, I can assure you that it is completely fictional. If you don't believe me, send me a self addressed stamped envelope along with proper request form, signed by the appropriate people with their authorization codes clearly marked. After your request is reviewed by the review committee, I will send you copies of the measurement sheets and flow charts used to create this story.

The Three Applicants to Gruff

Once upon a time there was a company called Gruff Inc. Gruff Inc. was a very large company. It was so large in fact, they had to employ a very tough Human Resources Director. It was the Director's job to be tough, demanding, and investigative when hiring new people. The Director was very good at his job and had the personality to match. Some even described his attitude as troll-like. Therefore, throughout the company, he had the nickname of, "The Troll".

On this particular day, The Troll was preparing to interview applicants for a job opening within Gruff Inc. Three applicants were waiting outside the office. Suddenly there was a knock at the door.

"Who's that knocking at my door?" asked The Troll.

"It is I, the first applicant to Gruff." In walked a well dressed man who appeared to be about 30 years old.

"And why do you think I should give you the job?" asked The Troll.

"Well," said the first applicant. "I have an MBA and 10 years of progressive experience with your direct competitor. I'm an expert in the industry and I am willing to share all the trade secrets I know about my former employer. Also, since I just won the lottery, I don't care what the salary is."

"Ha!" exclaimed The Troll. "I'm sick of you snot-nosed MBA's coming in here thinking you know so much about business. Big deal! You can read a balance sheet and you know what someone means when they say 'leveraged buyout'. I'll have you know that I eat MBA's for breakfast. We don't need your kind around here so get out now!"

(Fortunately, The Troll was in a good mood today because that could have been really bad.)

Soon, there was another knock at the door. "Who's that knocking at my door?" asked The Troll.

"It is I, the second applicant to Gruff." In walked an attractive woman who was also nicely dressed.

"And why do you think I should give you the job?" asked The Troll.

"Well," said the second applicant to Gruff, "I have my bachelors degree and several years experience in an unrelated industry but with very similar duties. I'm working on my masters degree in literature. I really think I am qualified for the job and I heard you offer a great salary and benefits."

"I am certainly impressed with your resume." said

The Troll. "Your margins are very nice and straight. You seem well qualified and I think you would fit in very nicely at our company. Let's see what Mr. 8-Ball (the original management consultant) has to say, shall we? Oh Mr. 8-ball....will this nice young lady get a job today? Sorry, the 8-ball says 'outlook not so good' so I guess you're out of luck. Now please be so kind as to leave my office and don't let the door hit you on the way out."

The Troll was feeling especially happy. This was turning out to be a great day. Soon, there was another knock at the door.

"Who's that knocking at my door?" asked The Troll.

"It is I, the third applicant to Gruff." In walked a casually dressed young man. He was wearing loafer shoes and a cartoon tie.

"And just what makes you think you're qualified

for the job?" asked The Troll.

"Well," said the third applicant to Gruff, "I just graduated with an associates degree in business. I have several years experience as a pizza delivery boy but I'm confident that I can make it in big business."

"Forget it!" said The Troll. "There is no way I would hire you into this company."

"Perhaps I should introduce myself," said the third applicant to Gruff. "I'm Larry Gruff. My father owns this company."

"Er, uh, um," stammered The Troll. "What I meant to say was there was no way I would hire you into this company on a measly 6 figure salary alone. Please, let me get you a company car and a corner office on the top floor. Also, you can have my membership to the golf club. I only go 3 or 4 times a week so I won't really miss it."

"I accept," said the third applicant to Gruff. And with that he was on his way to a successful career of delegating responsibility and empire building.

So it just goes to prove that if you have the right qualifications for the job, and present yourself properly in the interview, you can only succeed.

Little Red's
Riding Hoods

ong, long ago, in a place far, far away there lived a woman named Emily McClannihan.

While Emily was growing up her father had a job watering the big redwood trees. He was a big guy and had bright red hair. This earned him the nickname, Big Red. Emily was very close to her father and would follow him around everywhere. Sometimes she would even help out by watering some of the smaller redwoods. Eventually she got the nickname, Little Red.

Emily loved to ride horses. However she hated when the horse went full speed because her hair would get messed up. All her life she kept saying, "If only someone would design a good riding hood for me to wear, my hair wouldn't get messed up all the time."

When she was old enough, Little Red (remember, that's Emily) decided to go into business for herself selling riding hoods. She called her business 'Little Red's Riding Hoods' and she started down the road of entrepreneurship.

Little Red knew she was going to need help to get her business started, so she began looking for advice. Little Red spent quite a bit of money on books, magazines, videotapes, and computer software designed to tell her the "best" way to start her business. (Did you ever notice how none of these 'start-a-business' guides suggest buying 'start-a-business guides'? Hmmm, kinda makes you wonder.) Eventually, she chose to enlist the aid of the Small Business Administration.

While she was walking down the street one day, a man in a three-piece suit approached her from an alley.

"Psst, Lady. Wanna loan?" asked the man.

"Huh?" asked Little Red (such gripping dialog, don't you think?)

"My name is Peter Wolfe," said the man, "and I'm with First Solvent National Bank. Did you know that we have great rates on home equity loans right now? You can use the money for anything you want and the interest you pay might be tax deductible. You could even use the money to start a business. Also, if you sign up right now we'll give you free software that will let you file for bankruptcy from your personal computer at home."

"Golly!" said Little Red. (She is a master of linguistics, don't you agree?)

"Please!" said Mr. Wolfe. "I'm just starting out on this job. If I can just make a few more loans, they will give me a desk and a phone so I can work **inside** the building. I'll do anything for the business."

"Well," said Little Red in her usual eloquent manner, "I'm off to the see the Small Business Administration. I heard they can help me in my quest for money and power....I mean my desire to benefit others through a high quality, low cost, customer driven product."

"Is that what you think?" said Mr. Wolfe. "I'll get your loan yet, you'll see." And with that said, he ran off.

Little Red continued her journey to the SBA office. Soon she came across a dusty old storefront. The sign in the window, which appeared to be hand written, read "Small Biznuss Administrashun." Little Red went inside.

"Welcome," said the man inside. "Sorry about the mess, but our normal office had to be evacuated immediately. They think we may have a serious leak in our Ethernet and it's making everyone a little goofy. My name is Mr. Wol... er, Shark. How can I assist you today?"

"I want to start my own business and I'm here for a loan," said Little Red.

"Certainly," said Mr. Wol...er, Shark. "I just need you to fill out a few forms."

"My, what long applications you have," said Little Red.

"All the better to learn the inner most personal aspects of your past financial life, my dear," said Mr. Shark.

"My, what sharp pencils you have," said Little Red.

"All the better to compose the fine print, my dear," said Mr. Shark.

"And my, what large legal books you have," said Little Red.

"All the better to interpret the fine print, my dear," said Mr. Shark.

Suddenly, Little Red reached across the desk and pulled off a piece of masking tape that had been covering Mr. Shark's name tag.

"You're not Mr. Shark! You're Mr. Wolfe from the bank!" cried Little Red.

"Ha ha!" said Mr. Shark. "All you need to do now is sign here and I have your loan!"

Little Red was petrified. Mr. Shark chased her around the room with a pen yelling for her to sign. Suddenly, a construction worker opened the door and a big wind blew in. The loan papers flew off the desk, out to the street, and into the sewer... lost forever.

Little Red ran out of the building and eventually found her way to the real SBA office. After 2 years she finally had her loan and opened up 'Little Red's Riding Hoods.'

Unfortunately while she was arranging financing, a large corporation had taken hold of the market. It was impossible for her to compete against the tremendous marketing effort that had been put towards promoting *Cinderella's Glass Riding Hoods.*

(Now there is a lawsuit just waiting to happen.)

Little Red was forced to shut down her business. She eventually worked her way through college by donating plasma two times a week. Now she works as a mergers and acquisitions planner for a large, impersonal, corporate conglomerate.

Mr. Wolfe eventually got a desk and a phone. He is now hoping for a promotion that will give him enough status to have cubicle walls.

The construction worker got a severe paper cut in the incident and is resting comfortably at home thanks to a well-funded workers compensation policy.

This Space for Lease

The Lowly Employee

Once upon a time there was a huge corporate conglomerate that was very busy contributing to the free enterprise system of these United States. One day the CEO issued an order.

"I want a Business Plan. Who will write it?" asked the CEO.

"Not I," said the Senior Vice President. "I'll delegate it to the Vice President."

"Not I," said the Vice President. "The manager has more expertise in this area."

"Not I," said the Manager. He then turned to the lowly employee and said, "I know you have been wanting to take on more projects. I therefore empower you to do this one."

So the lowly employee started working on the business plan. It wasn't long before help was needed.

"Who will help me with the research?" said the lowly employee.

"I don't **do** research," said the Senior Vice President, "I analyze the results."

"I have reviewed the results of numerous studies done by some of the largest corporation's top management. These studies clearly demonstrate that research is more effective when done by those at the grass roots levels of the company," said the Vice President.

The Manager looked at the lowly employee and said, "Since you have access to the Internet, I think you are best equipped to handle the research."

The lowly employee worked long and hard gathering the research needed for the business plan. Many hours were spent in the library and on the Internet. Once the research was done, the lowly employee asked for help again.

"Who will write the plan?" asked the lowly employee.

"I don't **do** writing," said the Senior Vice President, "I analyze the writings of others."

"Sorry, my secretary is on vacation and I'm out of tapes for my Dictaphone," said the Vice President.

The Manager looked at the lowly employee and said, "My trained managerial eye noticed you have an MLA style handbook on your desk. My keen managerial instinct says to me, 'Hey, here is a person who likes to write.' I'm sure you'll do a great job."

So the lowly employee bought a word processing

package with his own money since the purchase request was denied. Apparently purchasing felt that word processing was just fancy typing and the company already had a large number of typewriters that were not realizing their full potential. After weeks of writing and revisions it was finally done.

"Who will help me with the graphics?" said the lowly employee.

"I don't **do** graphics," said the Senior Vice President, "I analyze the graphics done by others."

"I didn't get to the position I'm in by drawing pictures," said the Vice President.

The Manager looked at the lowly employee and said, "Here, I got this charting package at a trade show a few months ago. I hate to break the shrink wrap but I suppose this is as good a reason as any."

So the lowly employee loaded the graphics package onto a grossly underpowered PC and enrolled in a graphics design class at the local junior college. After weeks of intense work and study, the graphics were done and the business plan was complete.

"Who will present the plan?" asked the lowly employee.

"You've worked very hard, I'll relieve you of the burden and stress of preparing a presentation by doing it myself," said the Manager.

"You haven't had enough exposure to senior management and I wouldn't want you to get nervous and give a poor presentation. I had better take care of that for you," said the Vice President.

"I'm going to be in the Caribbean next week with the President for a board meeting. I'll let him beat me in a round of golf and then I'll present it to him while he is still in a good mood," said the Senior Vice President.

And so the Senior Vice President presented the business plan. The President loved the plan so much that it was implemented immediately without any modification. Within a month of operating under the new plan, profits were up 500%.

The Senior Vice President was rewarded with a large raise, more stock options, and a new company car. The Vice President was rewarded with a small raise and a corner office. The Manager was rewarded with a nice bonus check. The lowly employee received the prestigious "Employee of the Week" award and was given a paved parking space.

The moral of the story....As the trunk of the tree, you provide the strength and support for all that is above you. But take that away, and you realize you are just a stump.

The Little Accountant That Could

nce upon a time, there was an entry level accountant in a large, multi-national company. She had just graduated from college and had been on the job for only a few months.

On this particular morning, the Little Accountant came to work and found a memo on her desk that read, "Please put together a 5-year Pro forma statement for the entire company. You've got until the end of the week to complete it."

The Little Accountant was very concerned. She had never done anything like this before and had no idea how to start. She knew help was going to be necessary so she started by asking the company Controller.

"Can you help me with the Pro forma statement?" asked the Little Account.

"I'm too big and important to help with such a task," said the Controller who then shuffled off to a meeting.

The Little Accountant pressed on. She next asked the company's financial advisor.

"Can you help me with the Pro forma statement?" asked the Little Accountant.

"Sorry, the market is going wild and I have to contact our broker," said the financial advisor.

The Little Accountant was getting worried. Time was running out and something had to be done. Just then she passed her manager in the hall.

"Why are you out walking around?" asked the manager. "You have to get that Pro forma statement finished. The deadline has been moved up and now it has to be done today. Can you do it?"

"I suppose I could," said the Little Accountant. She then knew that it was up to her and her alone. And with that thought, she trotted off to her little cubicle.

"I suppose I could, I suppose I could, I suppose I could," the Little Accountant kept saying to herself as she worked very hard to get the job done.

After many hours of work and research she had completed the job. "I knew I could, I knew I could, I knew I could," said the Little Accountant.

Proudly the Little Accountant took the completed Pro forma statement to the Senior Staff for their review. As soon as the Pro forma was received, it was quickly filed away never to be seen again.

The Little Accountant learned a very valuable lesson that day which is also the moral of the story.

Even when the task seems beyond your abilities and you don't understand it, go ahead and do it anyway. Chances are, no one else understands it either and won't even look at it, so whatever you do will be just fine.

Little Miss Muffett

Little Miss Muffett,
Sat on her tuffett,
Her PC was churning away.
Along came a virus,
Wiped out her hard driveus,
And ruined her entire day.

Greedy Jack

Jack be greedy.
Jack buys quick.
Jack lost his money,
On one stock pick.

Hickory Dickory Dock

Hickory Dickory Dock.
The employees watched the clock.
The clock struck five.
They returned to their lives.
Hickory Dickory Dock.

Pees Porridge Hot

Pees porridge hot.
Pees porridge cold.
To be in the pees porridge futures market,
You must be very bold.
Sometimes it's hot.
Sometimes it's cold.
But you can make good money.
At least that's what we're told.

The Little Piggies

This little piggie played the market.
This little piggie liked CDs.
This little piggie had cash savings.
This little piggie had none.
And this little piggie played the lottery,
And what do you know, he won.

Humpty Dumpty

Humpty Dumpty sat on a wall.
Humpty Dumpty watched the DOW fall.
Despite safe investments,
And a shelter from tax,
They couldn't get Humpty,
Back in the black.

Itsy Bitsy Business

The itsy bitsy business
　picked up some market share.
Soon came the franchise to wipe
　them out of there.
Out came the Feds who said that
　isn't fair.
And the itsy bitsy business
　reclaimed their market share.

Ring Around The Lawyers

Ring around the lawyers,
A brief case full of cases,
Litigate, litigate, we all get sued.

The Woman Who Sold Shoes

There was an old woman,
    who used to sell shoes.
She had so many pairs,
    she didn't know what to do.
So she had a big sale.
Marked them all at half price.
The customers all loved her.
Now isn't that nice?

The Twelve Days of Business

On the First day of business, a customer gave to me,
    a dollar that I hung up on the wall.

On the Second day of business, a customer gave to me,
    two bounced checks,
    and a dollar that I hung up on the wall.

On the Third day of business a customer gave to me,
    three returned items,
    two bounced checks,
    and a dollar that I hung up on the wall.

On the Fourth day of business a customer gave to me,
> four stupid complaints,
> three returned items,
> two bounced checks,
> and a dollar that I hung up on the wall.

On the Fifth day of business a customer gave to me,
> five stolen credit cards,
> four stupid complaints,
> three returned items,
> two bounced checks,
> and a dollar that I hung up on the wall.

On the Sixth day of business a customer gave to me,
> six expired coupons,
> five stolen credit cards,
> four stupid complaints,
> three returned items,
> two bounced checks,
> and a dollar that I hung up on the wall.

On the Seventh day of business a customer gave to me,
> seven order changes,
> six expired coupons,
> five stolen credit cards,
> four stupid complaints,
> three returned items,
> two bounced checks,
> and a dollar that I hung on the wall.

On the Eighth day of business a customer gave to me,
> eight trips to the stock room,
> seven order changes,
> six expired coupons,
> five stolen credit cards,
> four stupid complaints,
> three returned items,
> two bounced checks,
> and a dollar that I hung up on the wall.

On the Ninth day of business a customer gave to me,
> nine gift certificates,
> eight trips to the stock room,
> seven order changes,
> six expired coupons,
> five stolen credit cards,
> four stupid complaints,
> three returned items,
> two bounced checks,
> and a dollar that I hung up on the wall.

On the Tenth day of business a customer gave to me,
> ten damaged pieces,
> nine gift certificates,
> eight trips to the stock room,
> seven order changes,
> six expired coupons,
> five stolen credit cards,
> four stupid complaints,
> three returned items,
> two bounced checks,
> and a dollar that I hung up on the wall.

On the Eleventh day of business a customer gave to me,
> eleven separate orders,
> ten damaged pieces,
> nine gift certificates,
> eight trips to the stock room,
> seven order changes,
> six expired coupons,
> five stolen credit cards,
> four stupid complaints,
> three returned items,
> two bounced checks,
> and a dollar that I hung up on the wall.

On the Twelfth day of business a customer gave to me,
>   twelve dollars in pennies,
>   eleven separate orders,
>   ten damaged pieces,
>   nine gift certificates,
>   eight trips to the stock room,
>   seven order changes,
>   six expired coupons,
>   five stolen credit cards,
>   four stupid complaints,
>   three returned items,
>   two bounced checks,
>   and a dollar that I hung up on the wall.

The Cat and the Fiddle

Hey diddle diddle, the cat sold his fiddle,
To an antique dealer in LA.
Sad he didn't know,
That he'd sold it too low,
But there wasn't much he could say.

If You're Profitable and You Know It

If you're profitable and you know it,
> clap your hands.

If you're profitable and you know it,
> clap your hands.

If you're profitable and you know it,
Then your margin ought to show it.
If you're profitable and you know it,
> clap your hands.

If the money's rolling in,
> clap your hands.

If the money's rolling in,
> clap your hands.

If you're swimming in the green,
Then that is pretty keen.
If the money's rolling in,
> clap your hands.

The Job Search Pokey

Put your resume in, take your resume out.
Put your resume in, and spread it all about.
You'll climb the corporate ladder,
Once you get yourself a job
That's what it's all about.

Put your best suit on.
Take your dress shoes out.
Put your best suit on,
And get the wrinkles out.
You have to dress the part,
If you want to get a job.
That's what it's all about.

Jack and the Bill

Jack took a bill, up the hill,
To pass some legislation.
Jack was able,
To pass money under the table,
And it was law with no hesitation.